Editor

Heather Douglas

Illustrator

Kelly McMahon

Cover Artist

Kevin Barnes

Editor in Chief

Ina Massler Levin, M.A.

Creative Director

Karen J. Goldfluss, M.S. Ed.

Art Coordinator

Renée Christine Yates

Imaging

James Edward Grace

Publisher

Mary D. Smith, M.S. Ed.

ITSY BITSY STORIES for Reading Comprehension

Short, high-interest stories that promote fluency, comprehension, and vocabulary development!

Author

Susan Mackey Collins, M. Ed.

Teacher Created Resources, Inc.

6421 Industry Way
Westminster, CA 92683
www.teachercreated.com

ISBN: 978-1-4206-3262-0

© 2009 Teacher Created Resources, Inc.
Made in U.S.A.

Teacher Created Resources

Table of Contents

Introduction

Reading is the foundation for all education. Practicing and exposing a child to a variety of reading opportunities is key to creating a successful reader. *Itsy Bitsy Stories for Reading Comprehension, Grade 2,* does just that.

Itsy Bitsy Stories for Reading Comprehension, Grade 2, is the perfect supplement to any reading program. The activities in this book are geared towards providing a variety of educational and entertaining fictional stories. These stories are short yet provide a high interest level for the reader. The activities in this book can be used successfully by any teacher in the regular classroom. The activities can also be used as homework to reinforce skills taught during the school day. This book has been written to help teach and reinforce important reading skills such as fluency, comprehension, and vocabulary. Teachers are sure to find a variety of ways to use this book in their classrooms.

Another feature with each reading passage in *Itsy Bitsy Stories for Reading Comprehension, Grade 2*, is the "Something Extra" activities which follow each story. For the teacher wishing to extend each reading opportunity, these activities provide yet another way to engage students even further in the joy of reading.

More Ideas for Teachers and Parents on How to Make the Most of This Book:

- Read aloud some of the stories.

- Have each student practice some of the activities on his or her own.

- Focus on key vocabulary words and take note of any words a student still needs to practice and learn.

- Review any work the student does on his or her own.

- Extend lessons by assigning extra stories for students who are ready to move forward.

Cal's Trip

Cal wanted to fly. He wished he could be like the birds in the sky. One day he went on vacation with his family. His family flew on a large plane. Cal loved flying up past the clouds. He was finally like the birds.

1. What did Cal want to do?

    a. Cal wanted to swim.

    b. Cal wanted to jump.

    c. Cal wanted to fly.

2. What animal did Cal want to be like?

    a. a kangaroo

    b. a bird

    c. a snake

3. How does Cal get to fly?

    a. He rides in a hot air balloon.

    b. He rides a roller coaster.

    c. He rides an airplane.

4. How does Cal feel about flying?

    a. He loves it.

    b. He does not like it.

    c. He thinks it is okay.

Something extra: If you could fly on a plane to another place, where would you go? On the lines below tell where you would fly to and why you would go there.

_____

_____

_____

_____

The Talking Bird

Gibb got a bird for his birthday. He wanted to teach his bird to talk. He tried to get his bird to say, "Birdie wants a cracker," but Birdie would not say it. One day Gibb was eating a cookie. "Birdie wants a cookie." Gibb could not believe it. Birdie could talk! He just didn't like crackers.

1. What does Gibb get for his birthday?

    a. a train set

    b. a pet bird

    c. a swing set

2. Gibb tries to teach his bird to

    a. talk

    b. fly

    c. swim

3. Gibb's bird does not like

    a. Gibb

    b. cookies

    c. crackers

4. By the end of the story Gibb's bird

    a. still can't talk

    b. eats lots of crackers

    c. can ask for cookies

Something extra: Pretend you have a pet bird that can talk. Write down three things you would teach your bird to say if you could. Remember, do not write anything that would hurt someone's feelings.

1. _____

2. _____

3. _____

Cloud Cover

Megan, the cow, could not sleep. The moon was much too <u>bright</u>. The clouds said, "Don't worry, Megan. We will help you get to sleep." The clouds moved carefully in front of the moon. Megan mooed her thanks to the clouds and went quickly to sleep.

1. What is wrong with Megan?

   a. She can't eat.

   b. She can't walk.

   c. She can't sleep.

2. What is keeping Megan awake?

   a. The tree frogs are too loud.

   b. The ground is too wet.

   c. The moon is too bright.

3. How do the clouds help Megan get to sleep?

   a. They cover the moon.

   b. They make a blanket for Megan.

   c. They don't help Megan at all.

4. In this story a word that means the opposite of <u>bright</u> is

   a. shiny

   b. dark

   c. light

Something extra: Imagine you are having trouble going to sleep. On the back of this page write a short story telling about your night. Remember to tell why you can't sleep. Be sure to explain how you finally do fall asleep.

Lucky Three

David wanted to learn to blow bubbles with his gum. He tried to make a bubble with one piece. Nothing happened. He tried to make a bubble with two pieces. Nothing happened. He added one more piece of gum. He made a bubble! Three was going to be his lucky number.

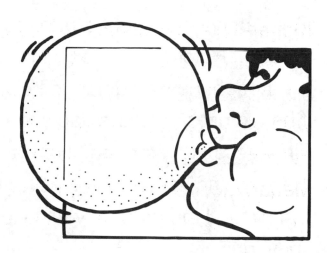

1. What does David wish he could do?

    a. make better grades at school

    b. stop biting his finger nails

    c. blow bubbles with his gum

2. What happens when David chews two pieces of bubble gum?

    a. He blows a huge bubble.

    b. He still cannot blow a bubble.

    c. He thinks he has too much gum in his mouth.

3. What is David's new lucky number?

    a. one

    b. two

    c. three

4. From this story you can guess that David is probably someone who

    a. gives up easily

    b. always keeps trying

    c. never tries very hard

Something extra: Think about something you tried and learned to do. In the space below tell about what it was and how you learned to do it.

_____

_____

Around and Around

The carnival ride went around and around. Peter did not feel very well. He thought he was going to be sick if he did not get off the ride soon. Finally the ride stopped. He was glad the spinning ride was over. Now he just wished the ground would stop spinning!

---

1. Where is the setting of this story?

    a. at the beach

    b. at the movie theater

    c. at the carnival

2. The ride Peter was on went

    a. up and down

    b. around and around

    c. back and forth

3. Peter wanted off the ride because

    a. he thought he was going to get sick

    b. he wanted to ride a different ride

    c. he was ready to leave the carnival

4. When Peter got off the ride

    a. he felt like the ground was still spinning

    b. he wanted to get right back on the ride

    c. he wanted to find his parents

Something extra: On the back of this page draw and color a picture of Peter at the carnival.

The Snow Sled

Snow was falling outside. Lane and Sam wanted to go outside and play but they had no sleds. Their father said, "Don't be sad. I'll get you each a sled." Their father came back with two lids from their trash cans. "Last one to the hill is a frozen snowman," their father said.

1. What do Lane and Sam want to do?

   a. play in the snow

   b. swim in the water

   c. ride in the car

2. Why can't Lane and Sam play in the snow?

   a. They do not have sleds.

   b. They do not have mittens.

   c. They do not like the snow.

3. What do the boys use as sleds?

   a. cardboard boxes

   b. trash can lids

   c. plastic bags

4. Something Lane and Sam might also do while playing in the snow is

   a. make a snowman

   b. read a book

   c. finish their homework

Something extra: On the back of this page draw and color a picture of Lane and Sam playing in the snow.

Wrong Day

Dwight did not want to get up for school. All he wanted to do was sleep. He finally got out of bed, got ready, grabbed his backpack, and went downstairs. His mother was already awake. She looked at Dwight and said, "Dwight, why are you dressed for school? It's Saturday!"

---

1. Dwight was feeling very

   a. sleepy

   b. happy

   c. sick

2. Dwight was too tired to go

   a. to baseball practice

   b. to school

   c. to the store

3. Dwight did not have to get up early because

   a. it was his birthday

   b. it was raining outside

   c. it was Saturday

4. What is one way Dwight could have known what day of the week it was?

   a. He could have looked in a dictionary.

   b. He could have looked in a mirror.

   c. He could have looked on a calendar.

Something extra: Think about the next Saturday that is coming up. What do you plan to do with your Saturday? On the back of this page write about your plans.

Sea Friends

Two beautiful mermaids lived in the sea. The two mermaids wished for some new friends to play with them. One day they met two giant sea turtles. The mermaids and the sea turtles swam and played all day long. Four new friends had fun in the sea.

1. What did the two mermaids wish for?

   a. a new place to live

   b. some better food

   c. new friends to play with them

2. What is the setting of this story?

   a. the park

   b. the sea

   c. the mountains

3. How do you know the mermaids had fun playing with the sea turtles?

   a. because they played together all day long

   b. because they gave each other their phone numbers

   c. because they were laughing and smiling a lot

4. How many creatures in the story became friends?

   a. four

   b. two

   c. three

Something extra: On the back of this page draw and color a picture of the mermaids and sea turtles playing together.

Playing Ball

Katie loved playing soccer with her friends. She wanted to score a goal for her team. The ball was coming <u>quickly</u> towards Katie. Katie kicked. She scored! Katie was glad she had helped her team.

1. What game does Katie love to play?

   a. softball

   b. volleyball

   c. soccer

2. Katie wants to help her team by

   a. running with the ball

   b. scoring a goal for the team

   c. cheering on the other players

3. The other players on Katie's team probably think Katie is

   a. a good player

   b. not a team player

   c. a bad player

4. A word that means the opposite of <u>quickly</u> is

   a. fast

   b. slowly

   c. speedy

Something extra: Katie likes to play soccer when she is not at school. What do you like to do when you are not in school? On the lines below write about what you like to do in your free time.

_____

_____

_____

_____

The Clubhouse

"Let's build a clubhouse in the back yard," Tina said. "What can we use to make our house?" Jack asked Tina. Just then Tina's mother brought a big, cardboard box outside with the trash. Tina and Jack both knew that was one box that would not be going in the trash.

1. What do Jack and Tina want to do?

   a. build a snowman

   b. build a teepee

   c. build a clubhouse

2. What problem do Jack and Tina have?

   a. They do not know what to do with their free time.

   b. They do not know what to use to make their clubhouse.

   c. They do not know what movie to watch on television.

3. Why do Tina and Jack think the box will not stay with the trash?

   a. They think the wind will blow the box away.

   b. They plan to use the box for their clubhouse.

   c. They think the neighbor will take the box.

4. A good title for this story might be

   a. A Box of Fun

   b. The Special Day

   c. Lost and Found

Something extra: Imagine you are starting a club in your own new clubhouse. What are some rules you would have for your new members? List three rules you would have for your club. Remember, do not hurt anyone's feelings or be rude to anyone when you are setting up your rules.

Rule 1: _____

Rule 2: _____

Rule 3: _____

High Jump

Steve wished he had a trampoline so he could jump and jump. Steve's family lived in an apartment so there was no yard for a trampoline. One day Steve's dad pulled the car in front of a store. "Where are we?" Steve asked his dad. "This is a place where kids can play on indoor jumpers. You can jump all day!"

1. Steve wishes he could have a

   a. go-cart

   b. swing set

   c. trampoline

2. Steve and his family live

   a. in an apartment

   b. in a house

   c. on a farm

3. Steve wants a trampoline so he can

   a. ride his bicycle on it

   b. jump on it

   c. sleep underneath it

4. Steve's dad takes him to a place where he can

   a. swim in a pool

   b. jump all day

   c. ride on skateboards

Something extra: List three words to tell how Steve probably feels when his father tells him he gets to jump all day.

1. _____

2. _____

3. _____

What Is It?

Kelly and Thomas were playing outside. They <u>heard</u> a noise in the woods right behind their house. What could it be? Out came their dog, Princess. Kelly and Thomas were sure glad to see their own dog!

1. Where were Kelly and Thomas playing?

   a. outside their house

   b. at their school

   c. at the park

2. When Kelly and Thomas heard the noise in the woods they probably felt

   a. scared

   b. happy

   c. sad

3. In this story the word <u>heard</u> means

   a. a group of animals

   b. to listen to something

   c. a type of vegetable

4. What made the noise behind their yard?

   a. a cat

   b. a squirrel

   c. a dog

Something extra: In this story Kelly and Thomas have a dog named Princess. In the space below make a list of names you might give a pet. Then circle the three you like best.

_____   _____

_____   _____

_____   _____

Spooky Spider

Chris needed his ball that was in his closet. He was afraid to get it. He had seen a spider in his closet just last night. He did not know where the spider had gone. Chris saw another ball on his dresser. He smiled. He wouldn't have to worry about the spider after all.

1. What did Chris need?

    a. a haircut

    b. a book

    c. a ball

2. Why was Chris afraid to look in his closet?

    a. He thought there might be a snake in his closet.

    b. He thought his closet was too messy.

    c. He thought there might be a spider in his closet.

3. What would be a good reason that Chris might need a ball?

    a. Chris might need a ball to play a game.

    b. Chris might need a ball to go to sleep.

    c. Chris might need a ball to do his homework.

4. Where does Chris find a ball?

    a. in the garage

    b. in his bedroom

    c. in his front yard

Something extra: Everyone is afraid sometimes. Chris is afraid of the spider. Have you ever been afraid of something? List one thing that is a little scary to you. Tell why it is scary to you.

_____

_____

The Chase

One day a rabbit was being chased by a fox. The rabbit was scared, but he was also smart. "There is more food than just me in this hole," Rabbit told Fox. Fox was <u>greedy</u> and looked in the hole. Rabbit snuck out the other end and pushed Fox into the hole and ran quickly away.

1. The rabbit in this story is being chased by a

   a. fox

   b. dog

   c. cat

2. Why is the rabbit scared?

   a. The rabbit is lost.

   b. The rabbit thinks the fox might eat him.

   c. The rabbit thinks he will run out of food for the winter.

3. In this story the word <u>greedy</u> means

   a. to act silly

   b. to sing loudly

   c. to want more

4. The rabbit was able to get away from the fox because

   a. he tricked the fox

   b. he ran faster than the fox

   c. he had friends who helped him

Something extra: The rabbit in this story is very smart. Think about someone famous you have learned about in school or someone you know outside of school who is very smart. On the lines below tell who that someone is and write a few sentences about him or her.

_____

_____

_____

Hide-and-Seek

Peter and Lisa were playing hide-and-seek. Lisa was it. She couldn't find Peter in any of the places she looked.

Lisa was ready to give up. Then she saw a pair of shoes sticking out from behind the curtains. "Found you," Lisa said. "Now you are it!"

---

1. What game are Peter and Lisa playing?

    a. freeze tag

    b. hide-and-seek

    c. kick the can

2. What problem did Lisa have?

    a. She was hungry.

    b. She wanted to be the person to hide.

    c. She couldn't find Peter.

3. Lisa finds Peter when she sees his

    a. hand

    b. shoes

    c. face

4. Peter is hiding behind

    a. the sofa

    b. the door

    c. the curtains

Something extra: Lisa and Peter like to play hide-and-seek. What is a game you like to play? On the lines below tell about your favorite game.

_____

_____

_____

The Bus Ride

Carl had never ridden the school bus. He was a little scared. What if he missed the bus? What if the driver forgot to let him off the bus? Mr. Mason, the bus driver, smiled and told Carl he would make sure he got on the bus and got home safely. Carl was glad Mr. Mason was his bus driver.

1. Carl had never ridden

   a. on a train

   b. on a bicycle

   c. on a school bus

2. One thing Carl worried about was that he might

   a. forget his lunch on the bus

   b. miss his bus

   c. get sick on the bus

3. Mr. Mason, the bus driver, is a very _____ man.

   a. kind

   b. mean

   c. angry

4. How does Carl feel about Mr. Mason being his bus driver?

   a. He is glad he is his bus driver.

   b. He does not like him being his bus driver.

   c. He wishes he had a different bus driver.

Something extra: Imagine you could add something to the school bus to make it better. What would you add? Would you put televisions on every bus? Would you have seats that slide back? Be creative. List your idea or ideas on the back of this page.

Candy's Apple

"I am hungry," said Candy, the horse. "I wish the farmer would bring me my food." Candy did not see the farmer anywhere. Candy did see a tree on the other side of the fence. Candy stretched her neck and reached the tree. It was filled with apples. Candy wasn't hungry anymore.

1. In this story the main character is a

   a. goat

   b. cow

   c. horse

2. Candy's problem is that she is

   a. sleepy

   b. upset

   c. hungry

3. Candy is waiting for _____ to bring her some food.

   a. her friends

   b. the farmer

   c. the farmer's wife

4. Candy isn't hungry after she eats

   a. some carrots

   b. some peaches

   c. some apples

Something extra: Candy likes to eat apples. Many people like to eat apples, too. There are many different types of apples. With your teacher's permission, bring some apples to class. Make sure you know what type of apples you are bringing to school. Let the teacher divide the apples among the students to find out what type of apples everyone likes. Write the name of the apple you liked best on the following line:

_____

Fun in the Dark

Timmy was afraid of the storm. He was staying up with his mother and father. All of a sudden the lights went off. It was so dark. Timmy's dad turned on a flashlight. He taught Timmy how to make shadow puppets on the wall. He used his hands and a flashlight to make the puppets. Timmy smiled. Stormy nights weren't so bad after all.

1. Why was Timmy afraid?

   a. He did not like storms.

   b. He heard a strange noise.

   c. He was alone in the house.

2. Timmy's father helped him forget about the storm by

   a. telling Timmy some stories

   b. teaching Timmy how to make shadow puppets

   c. telling Timmy to go to sleep

3. The next time it storms, Timmy will probably

   a. want to roast marshmallows

   b. want to sleep with his mother and father

   c. want to make shadow puppets

4. A good title for this story might be

   a. Don't Be Afraid

   b. Noises in the Dark

   c. Summer Fun

Something extra: With your teacher's help, try making some shadow puppets of your own. After the teacher has darkened the room, use a flashlight or an overhead projector to make a spotlight on the wall. You will make your puppets by placing your hand or hands in front of the light on the wall. Place your hands in different positions to create different animals. For example, make one hand into a fist. Then lift your pointer and middle finger into a V sign. Place it in front of the light and look on the wall. You have made a rabbit!

Pirate's Dream

Timmy was on a pirate's ship. Waves shook and rocked the boat. The boat shook harder. Timmy opened his eyes and saw his mother. She was gently shaking him awake. Timmy hugged his mother. He was glad it had all been a dream.

1. Timmy dreamed that he was

   a. on an airplane

   b. on a ship

   c. on a train

2. How did Timmy's dream make him feel?

   a. The dream made Timmy feel happy.

   b. The dream made Timmy feel scared.

   c. The dream made Timmy feel angry.

3. Who or what woke Timmy from his dream?

   a. his father

   b. his alarm clock

   c. his mother

4. What probably made Timmy dream the boat was rocking?

   a. His mother was trying to wake him.

   b. His stomach was hurting.

   c. He was in the middle of an earthquake.

Something extra: Imagine you are a pirate on a ship. On the back of this page draw and color a picture of you as a pirate. Don't forget to give yourself a good pirate name!

Lost and Found

Cindy's mother could not find her glasses. She was scared she had left them at the store. She turned and asked Cindy if she knew where her glasses might be. Cindy pointed to the top of her mother's head. "I've found your glasses, Mom. Oh, and if you need a pencil, be sure to check behind your ear."

---

1. Cindy's mother could not find her
   _____.

   a. purse

   b. wallet

   c. glasses

2. Where did Cindy's mother think she had left her glasses?

   a. at Cindy's school

   b. at the store

   c. at home

3. Where did Cindy find her mother's glasses?

   a. in her mother's purse

   b. in her mother's car

   c. on her mother's head

4. What else did Cindy find while looking for her mother's glasses?

   a. some money

   b. a pencil

   c. a gift card

Something extra: Pretend Cindy's mother has not found her glasses. On the back of this page draw and color a "Lost and Found" sign for Cindy's mother's glasses. Be sure to tell what the glasses look like, give a phone number where someone can be reached, and offer a reward for the missing glasses. Remember, you want people to notice your sign so do a good job on it!

Fly So High

Once upon a time there was a fairy princess. The fairy princess was scared to fly. Her friends the butterflies told her they would fly with her. She was scared but she tried flying with her friends. It was not long before she could fly, and she was no longer scared. The fairy princess thanked her good friends.

---

1. Why was the fairy princess scared?

   a. She was scared to fly.

   b. She was scared of the butterflies.

   c. She was scared of her shadow.

2. Who taught the fairy princess to fly without being scared?

   a. the other fairies

   b. the bumble bees

   c. the butterflies

3. By the end of the story, how does the fairy princess feel about flying?

   a. She is still afraid.

   b. She does not like to fly.

   c. She is no longer scared to fly.

4. A good title for this story might be

   a. Flying Lessons

   b. Driving Lessons

   c. Singing Lessons

Something extra: With your teacher's help create a beautiful butterfly. Take a white piece of paper and fold it in half like a card. On only one half of the paper, drip different colors of paint. Fold the paper together and carefully press the two sides. Next, open the paper. There will be identical images on both sides. Let the paint dry. Then draw an outline around the design to make wings. Add a body for the butterfly down the seam of the paper. Finally, add a face and antennae for your butterfly.

Randy's Loose Tooth

"My tooth won't come out, but it is very loose," Randy told his brother, Bill. "I know what to do," Bill said. Bill gave Randy an apple and told him to take a big bite. Randy did. He looked and saw his tooth was in the apple and out of his mouth. "I guess an apple a day really is a good thing," Randy said.

1. What is Randy's problem?

   a. He needs to make his bed.

   b. He is scared he will not make the soccer team.

   c. His loose tooth will not come out.

2. Who does Randy ask to help him?

   a. his mother

   b. his sister

   c. his brother

3. What happens when Randy bites into the apple?

   a. He finds a worm.

   b. He spits out the apple.

   c. His tooth comes out of his mouth.

4. A word that means the opposite of loose is

   a. tight

   b. baggy

   c. goose

Something extra: On the back of this page draw and color a picture of you with at least one tooth missing.

Snack Attack

Austin and his brothers were hungry. They went to the kitchen to make a <u>snack</u>. They all wanted peanut butter on bread. They pulled out the loaf of bread and the peanut butter. Oh no! There was only one piece of bread left. Austin said, "Let's share by cutting the bread into three pieces." The brothers all enjoyed their slightly smaller snack.

---

1. Austin and his brothers wanted to make _____.

   a. a snack

   b. their beds

   c. good grades

2. How many pieces of bread were there?

   a. three

   b. two

   c. one

3. How do the brothers solve their problem?

   a. Austin and his brothers share the piece of bread.

   b. Austin and his brothers do not eat anything.

   c. Austin and his brothers go to the store.

4. The word <u>snack</u> means

   a. a short nap

   b. a small meal

   c. a funny joke

Something extra: Think about a time you shared something with someone else. On the back of this paper write about what you shared. Be ready to share your story with the class.

Night Troubles

Mack could not go to sleep. His mother came into his room. She had something in her hand. It was Mack's special blanket. She tucked him in with his special blanket. Mack could not keep his eyes open any longer.

1. What was wrong with Mack?

    a. He could not stop crying.

    b. He could not find his mother.

    c. He could not go to sleep.

2. How did Mack's mother help him get to sleep?

    a. She brought him his blanket.

    b. She gave him his teddy bear.

    c. She turned on his light.

3. How did Mack feel when he got his special blanket?

    a. sad

    b. silly

    c. glad

4. How does the reader know Mack finally went to sleep?

    a. He starts snoring.

    b. He cannot keep his eyes open.

    c. He talks in his sleep.

Something extra: What do you think Mack's special blanket looks like? On the back of this page draw and color a picture of Mack sleeping with his special blanket.

World Wise

Nancy and James wanted to help the earth. They told everyone they knew to give their soda cans to them. They would help by <u>recycling</u> cans. Soon they had enough cans to get recycled. Nancy and James were glad they had found a way to help.

1. Who or what do Nancy and James want to help?

   a. their teacher

   b. their families

   c. the earth

2. How are Nancy and James going to help the earth?

   a. They are going to recycle cans.

   b. They are going to recycle plastic.

   c. They are going to recycle paper.

3. In this story the word <u>recycling</u> most likely means

   a. to throw away

   b. to use again

   c. to buy more things

4. One thing, besides recycling, that people might do to help the earth is

   a. stop littering

   b. stop singing

   c. stop learning

Something extra: Pretend your school is starting a new program to recycle items. On the back of this page draw and color a poster telling people about the new program.

Big Sister

Emma's mother was going to have a baby. Emma <u>hoped</u> she would be a good big sister. "Emma, come here. I have a surprise for you," Emma's mother said. Emma's mother gave her a T-shirt. "#1 Big Sister" was written on the shirt. Emma knew her mother believed in her. She was going to be a great big sister.

---

1. Emma and her family are going to get

   a. a new pet

   b. a new house

   c. a new baby

2. What is Emma's surprise?

   a. a backpack

   b. a T-shirt

   c. a pair of shoes

3. Why is the shirt special to Emma?

   a. The shirt says she will be a good big sister.

   b. The shirt is in her favorite color.

   c. The shirt is from her favorite store.

4. In this story the word <u>hoped</u> means

   a. to jump around

   b. to want something

   c. to scream and shout

Something extra: In this story Emma gets a shirt that says something special about her. On the back of this page draw and color a shirt that says something special about you. Write something on the front of the shirt that tells about something you do well. For example, "Fantastic Artist" or "Straight A Student." Don't be afraid to say something great about yourself!

Daisy's Garden

Daisy liked working in her garden. One day she was outside pulling weeds out from around her plants. She saw a snake. Daisy was not afraid. She knew it was just a harmless garden snake. She stopped pulling weeds and waited for the snake to move on. Once it left, Daisy went back to enjoying her garden.

1. What is one thing Daisy likes to do?

    a. Daisy likes to read books.

    b. Daisy likes to make crafts.

    c. Daisy likes to work in her garden.

2. What are two things Daisy sees in her garden?

    a. a friend and plants

    b. butterflies and flowers

    c. a snake and weeds

3. Why is Daisy not afraid of the snake?

    a. She knows it will not harm her.

    b. She does not see the snake.

    c. She thinks the snake is a lizard.

4. Daisy is probably a person who

    a. does not like animals

    b. likes animals

    c. does not like being outside

Something extra: On the back of this page draw and color a picture of the snake in Daisy's garden.

Report Card Day

Kat was glad to be home from school. Kat's teacher told her not to open her report card until she got home. Kat gave her parents her report card. They took it out of the envelope and opened the report card. "We are so proud of you," Kat's mother said. "You have straight A's. Tonight we will bake a cake to celebrate your wonderful grades!"

---

1. Why did Kat not open her report card?

   a. She was scared she had a bad grade.

   b. She did not want to see her grades.

   c. Her teacher told her not to open her report card.

2. How did Kat's parents feel about her grades?

   a. They did not like her grades.

   b. They were very proud of her grades.

   c. They were upset with Kat about her grades.

3. Kat's mother tells her they will celebrate by

   a. going to the movies

   b. not doing anymore homework

   c. baking a cake

4. Kat got _____ on her report card.

   a. A's and B's

   b. A's, B's, and C's

   c. All A's

Something extra: Imagine your teacher had to write a note on your report card. What would the note say? On the back of this page write a note home that could be on your very own report card.

Star Shine

"I wish I could shine brighter," the tiny star said to the bigger star. "Someone must make a wish on you," said the bigger star. "When that happens, you will <u>shine</u> bright." All of a sudden the little star started to glow brighter. The little star smiled. "Someone is getting his wish and so am I!"

1. What does the tiny star want to do?

   a. fall from the sky

   b. grow larger

   c. shine brighter

2. What will happen if someone makes a wish on the tiny star?

   a. The star will shine brighter.

   b. The star will become a planet.

   c. The star will shine less.

3. The word <u>shine</u> means

   a. glow

   b. stare

   c. hit

4. In this story the _____ gets its wish to come true.

   a. the moon

   b. the tiny star

   c. the bigger star

Something extra: A night sky is beautiful with all the stars shining brightly. On the back of this page draw and color a night sky. Don't forget to include the tiny star getting its wish!

Creature of the Sea

Amanda and Mark were walking on the beach. Amanda saw something in the water. It was a shell. She picked up the shell to show it to Mark. Suddenly she felt the shell move in her hand. Inside the shell was a small sea creature. The shell was its home. Mark told Amanda to put the animal back in the water. Amanda and Mark watched the animal until it was gone from their sight.

---

1. Where is the setting of this story?

   a. in a park

   b. in the mountains

   c. at the beach

2. What does Amanda see in the water?

   a. She sees a starfish.

   b. She sees some seaweed.

   c. She sees a shell.

3. What is inside the shell?

   a. nothing

   b. a sea creature

   c. water

4. Why would a sea animal be inside a shell?

   a. The shell is stuck on its back.

   b. The shell is its home.

   c. The shell is very pretty.

Something extra: On the back of this page draw and color a picture of you at the beach.

Good Cooking

"Let's play a game," Dad said to his children. "What will we play, Dad?" the children asked. "Let's play restaurant," said Dad. All the kids loved playing restaurant, but they really liked making the fancy desserts. The best part of the game was eating what they had cooked!

---

1. What game does Dad want to play?

   a. cards

   b. checkers

   c. restaurant

2. The children in the story feel _____ about playing restaurant.

   a. happy

   b. sad

   c. upset

3. The children like to play with dad because

   a. they get to eat what they have cooked

   b. they get to run and hide

   c. they get to skip their chores

4. The father in this story probably enjoys

   a. playing the piano

   b. cooking with his family

   c. watching a lot of television

Something extra: What is your favorite food to eat? Try writing a recipe for your favorite dish. Use the back of this page to list the ingredients. Then list any directions needed for making your special treat.

Frozen Treat

"I wish I had some ice cream," Patty said. "We don't have any ice cream," Patty's mother said, "but I know how we can get something cold and frozen that tastes good." Patty's mother got out some juice. She poured juice into a cup and put a plastic spoon in the cup. Then she put the cup in the freezer. "Soon you will have a great, frozen treat!"

---

1. Patty wishes she had some

   a. dolls

   b. ice cream

   c. video games

2. Who helps Patty with her problem?

   a. Patty helps herself.

   b. Patty's sister helps her.

   c. Patty's mother helps her.

3. What is Patty's mother making for Patty?

   a. She is making a pizza.

   b. She is making a frozen treat.

   c. She is making a mess.

4. What did Patty's mother put in the cup?

   a. a spoon and some juice

   b. an ice cube and some juice

   c. ice cream and a spoon

Something extra: Ice cream is one way to cool down on a hot day. In the space below list three more ways you can cool down on a hot day.

Ways to Cool Down on a Hot Day:

1. _____

2. _____

3. _____

Animal Sounds

The lions were roaring. The snakes were hissing. The ducks were quacking. The animals at the zoo were all saying hello to their new friend. Mother Hippo had a baby girl!

1. The snakes in this story are

   a. sleeping

   b. eating

   c. hissing

2. The animals in this story all live

   a. in the park

   b. in the woods

   c. in the zoo

3. Why are all the animals talking?

   a. Someone is visiting the zoo.

   b. Mother Hippo had a baby.

   c. It is time to eat.

4. A good title for this story might be

   a. Mother Hippo Makes New Friends

   b. New Baby at the Zoo

   c. Visiting the Animals

Something extra: In this story Mother Hippo has a baby. Babies are so cute! In the space below draw and color a picture of what you think you looked like as a baby.

Stop Running

Alex and Kay were running through the house. "Stop running," their mother said. All of a sudden Alex and Kay slid across the floor and fell! They looked up and saw their mother. She had a mop and a bucket of water. "Maybe you two should listen a little more and run a little less," their mother said with a smile.

---

1. Alex and Kay should not have been

   a. eating a snack

   b. playing outside

   c. running in the house

2. Why is the floor wet?

   a. Alex has spilled juice

   b. Mom has been mopping the floor.

   c. Mom has spilled her bucket of water.

3. Why should Alex and Kay listen better?

   a. They need to keep themselves safe.

   b. They need to hear the television.

   c. They need to do better in school.

4. A good title for this story might be

   a. Listen and Learn

   b. Kid's Day

   c. Summer Fun

Something extra: What if Alex and Kay had listened to their mother? What if they had stopped running in the house? How would the story have ended? On the back of this page write a new ending for this story.

Dr. Tom

Dr. Tom was Jake's dentist. Jake's
sister Sophie had never been to the
dentist. Jake told Sophie that Dr. Tom
was a very nice man. At the dentist's
office Jake took Sophie back to meet
Dr. Tom. The dentist told Sophie she
could pick out a movie. She could
watch it while he looked at her teeth.
The screen would be on the ceiling.
Sophie decided she liked going to the
dentist.

1. What type of job does Dr. Tom have?

   a. He is a family doctor.

   b. He is a veterinarian.

   c. He is a dentist.

2. Sophie is Jake's

   a. best friend

   b. cousin

   c. sister

3. At the dentist's office, Sophie could watch

   a. Jake getting his teeth checked

   b. herself in the mirror

   c. a movie on the ceiling

4. After her visit, Sophie decides

   a. she is scared of the dentist

   b. she does not like going to the dentist

   c. she likes going to the dentist

Something extra: Find a partner in the room. Then on the back of your own
paper, take turns drawing each other's smile. Have your partner smile so you
can see his or her teeth. Remember, you are not drawing the person's face; you
are only drawing his or her picture-perfect smile.

Something New

"We are going to try something <u>new</u> for supper," Jan's mother said. Jan was not very happy. Her mom was not a very good cook. Jan's mother put a pizza box on the table. "I bought a pizza from a new pizza place," Jan's mother said. "Now do you like my 'something new,' Jan?"

1. What surprise does Jan's mother have for Jan?

    a. She is getting Jan a puppy.

    b. She and Jan are trying something new for supper.

    c. She is giving Jan a new toy.

2. Jan thinks her mother is not very good at

    a. singing

    b. cooking

    c. swimming

3. A good title for this story might be

    a. My Friend Jan

    b. Supper Surprise

    c. Great Dessert

4. In this story the word <u>new</u> means

    a. something that is in a newspaper

    b. something that is different

    c. something that is the same as before

Something extra: On the back of this page draw and color a picture of you and your parents (or someone close to you) doing something new together. Be ready to tell the class about your picture.

Small Problem

Kaitlyn and Kristen wanted to ride the roller coaster. The man in charge of the roller coaster told them they were too short to ride. The girls went and watched the ride take off without them. The roller coaster stopped at the top of the hill. It was stuck! Kristen said to Kaitlyn, "Maybe being little isn't such a bad thing after all."

1. What do Kaitlyn and Kristen want to do?

   a. go down the water slide

   b. ride the roller coaster

   c. go see a movie

2. Why can't the girls ride the roller coaster?

   a. They are not old enough.

   b. They do not have enough money.

   c. They are not tall enough.

3. Why are Kaitlyn and Kristen glad they did not get to ride the roller coaster?

   a. The roller coaster stops working.

   b. The roller is not a lot of fun to ride.

   c. It is time for them to go home.

4. Kristen thinks being small might be

   a. a good thing

   b. a bad thing

   c. a silly thing

Something extra: Some people are very small. Some people are very tall. Other people are in the middle. On the back of this page draw and color a picture of the smallest person you can draw. Then beside the person you have drawn, use as much of your paper as you can to draw the tallest person you can draw.

Pizza Possible

Shelby wanted pizza for lunch. Her father told her they did not have any pizza. Her father went to the refrigerator. He pulled out a can of biscuits, some cheese, and some tomato sauce. "We do not have a pizza already made. But, we can make our own," he said to Shelby. Shelby just loved her dad's great ideas.

1. What does Shelby want for lunch?

   a. a hamburger

   b. a pizza

   c. a sandwich

2. What does Shelby's father tell her they will do?

   a. make their own pizzas

   b. order out for pizza

   c. go to a restaurant for pizza

3. Shelby thought her father's idea was

   a. good

   b. silly

   c. bad

4. Shelby and her father probably

   a. get along very well with each other

   b. do not spend much time together

   c. do not like pizza very much

Something extra: Shelby's father was very nice to Shelby. He is helping her make a pizza. What is something nice you could do for someone? Think about what you could do, and then write about it on the back of this page.

Up and Away

Hunter went to the space museum. He loved looking at all the rockets. He knew he wanted to fly in space when he got older. That night his parents told him he would be flying on a plane to go and visit his grandparents. Hunter was so happy about getting to fly. He knew it wasn't a rocket, but it was a start!

---

1. At the space museum Hunter likes to look at

    a. the rockets

    b. the moon rocks

    c. the telescopes

2. When Hunter is older he wants to

    a. work on a farm

    b. fix cars and trucks

    c. fly in space

3. Hunter is going to get to fly

    a. in a hot air balloon

    b. in a rocket ship

    c. in an airplane

4. How does Hunter feel about getting to fly?

    a. He is very excited.

    b. He is not at all excited.

    c. He is upset because it is a plane and not a rocket ship.

Something extra: Hunter wants to fly into space when he is older. What do you want to do when you are older? Think about all the things you can be or do. Then make a list of them on the back of this page.

Ride Again

Jennifer and Tim were at the water park. Jennifer wanted to ride the <u>tall</u> slide, but she was scared. Tim told Jennifer that he would go with her down the slide. Jennifer and Tim had so much fun. They both wanted to go on the slide again and again.

1. Where were Jennifer and Tim spending their day?

   a. at school

   b. at the library

   c. at the water park

2. What did Jennifer want to ride?

   a. all of the rides

   b. the tall water slide

   c. the roller coaster

3. How did Jennifer feel about the ride after she rode it?

   a. She loved it.

   b. She did not like it.

   c. She thought it was okay.

4. In this story a word that means the opposite of <u>tall</u> is

   a. small

   b. big

   c. large

Something extra: The water slide Jennifer wants to ride is very tall. What are some things that are big or tall to you? In the space below list at least four things that are very tall to you.

1. _____

2. _____

3. _____

4. _____

Play Time for Jillian

Jillian was playing by herself on the swing set. She fell off the swing and hurt her knee. Jillian's mother came and kissed her on the cheek. Jillian felt better and was now ready to play some more.

1. Who was Jillian playing with in this story?

   a. Jillian was playing with her sister.

   b. Jillian was playing with her cousin.

   c. Jillian was playing by herself.

2. Where was Jillian playing?

   a. on the swing set

   b. in her bedroom

   c. in a swimming pool

3. How did Jillian's mother help her feel better?

   a. She gave her a lollipop.

   b. She bought her a toy.

   c. She gave her a kiss.

4. A good title for this story might be

   a. Jillian Gets Hurt

   b. Jillian and Her Friends

   c. Jillian Saves the Day

Something extra: There are many types of swing sets. On the back of this sheet, draw and color the perfect swing set. Finish the sentence below and tell why your swing set is so great.

My swing set is great because _____

_____

_____

The Lemonade Stand

Mary opened a lemonade <u>stand</u> in her front yard. Mrs. Smith, Mary's neighbor, came outside. She asked Mary if she could buy all of her lemonade. Mrs. Smith was having a party at her house. She said that the lemonade would be perfect for her party. Mary could not help but wish that Mrs. Smith would have a party every day!

1. What was Mary selling at her stand?

   a. ice pops

   b. toys

   c. lemonade

2. In this story the word <u>stand</u> is most like the word

   a. store

   b. sit

   c. house

3. Why did Mrs. Smith want to buy Mary's lemonade?

   a. Mrs. Smith was very thirsty.

   b. Mrs. Smith wanted to close Mary's lemonade stand.

   c. Mrs. Smith wanted the lemonade for her party.

4. Why did Mary wish Mrs. Smith would have a party every day?

   a. so she could sell more lemonade

   b. so she could go to the party

   c. so she could get a new outfit for the party

Something extra: Pretend Mrs. Smith has sent out invitations to her party. On the back of this sheet draw and color an invitation to the party. Be sure and tell everyone invited there will be plenty of lemonade at the party.

Answer Sheets

Student Name: _____

Title of Reading Passage: _____

1. (a) (b) (c)   3. (a) (b) (c)

2. (a) (b) (c)   4. (a) (b) (c)

Student Name: _____

Title of Reading Passage: _____

1. (a) (b) (c)   3. (a) (b) (c)

2. (a) (b) (c)   4. (a) (b) (c)

Answer Key

Page 4: Cal's Trip
1. c
2. b
3. c
4. a

Page 5: The Talking Bird
1. b
2. a
3. c
4. c

Page 6: Cloud Cover
1. c
2. c
3. a
4. b

Page 7: Lucky Three
1. c
2. b
3. c
4. b

Page 8: Around and Around
1. c
2. b
3. a
4. a

Page 9: The Snow Sled
1. a
2. a
3. b
4. a

Page 10: Wrong Day
1. a
2. b
3. c
4. c

Page 11: Sea Friends
1. c
2. b
3. a
4. a

Page 12: Playing Ball
1. c
2. b
3. a
4. b

Page 13: The Clubhouse
1. c
2. b
3. b
4. a

Page 14: High Jump
1. c
2. a
3. b
4. b

Page 15: What Is It?
1. a
2. a
3. b
4. c

Page 16: Spooky Spider
1. c
2. c
3. a
4. b

Page 17: The Chase
1. a
2. b
3. c
4. a

Page 18: Hide-and-Seek
1. b
2. c
3. b
4. c

Page 19: The Bus Ride
1. c
2. b
3. a
4. a

Page 20: Candy's Apple
1. c
2. c
3. b
4. c

Page 21: Fun in the Dark
1. a
2. b
3. c
4. a

Page 22: Pirate's Dream
1. b
2. b
3. c
4. a

Page 23: Lost and Found
1. c
2. b
3. c
4. b

Page 24: Fly So High
1. a
2. c
3. c
4. a

Page 25: Randy's Loose Tooth
1. c
2. c
3. c
4. a

Page 26: Snack Attack
1. a
2. c
3. a
4. b

Answer Key *(cont.)*

Page 27: Night Troubles
1. c
2. a
3. c
4. b

Page 28: World Wise
1. c
2. a
3. b
4. a

Page 29: Big Sister
1. c
2. b
3. a
4. b

Page 30: Daisy's Garden
1. c
2. c
3. a
4. b

Page 31: Report Card Day
1. c
2. b
3. c
4. c

Page 32: Star Shine
1. c
2. a
3. a
4. b

Page 33: Creature of the Sea
1. c
2. c
3. b
4. b

Page 34: Good Cooking
1. c
2. a
3. a
4. b

Page 35: Frozen Treat
1. b
2. c
3. b
4. a

Page 36: Animal Sounds
1. c
2. c
3. b
4. b

Page 37: Stop Running
1. c
2. b
3. a
4. a

Page 38: Dr. Tom
1. c
2. c
3. c
4. c

Page 39: Something New
1. b
2. b
3. b
4. b

Page 40: Small Problem
1. b
2. c
3. a
4. a

Page 41: Pizza Possible
1. b
2. a
3. a
4. a

Page 42: Up and Away
1. a
2. c
3. c
4. a

Page 43: Ride Again
1. c
2. b
3. a
4. a

Page 44: Play Time for Jillian
1. c
2. a
3. c
4. a

Page 45: The Lemonade Stand
1. c
2. a
3. c
4. a